FROG'S WINTER WALK

Written by Jessica Schaub & Illustrated by Sarah Aman

Text Copyright © 2013 by Jessica Schaub

Illustrations Copyright © 2013 by Sarah Aman

All rights reserved. This book or any portion thereof may not be reproduced or used in any manner whatsoever without the express written permission of the publisher except for the use of brief quotations in a book review.

First Printing, 2013

ISBN: 978-0-9897039-0-1

Children's Illustrated Fiction

Printed in the United States of America

King Books Publishing

KING BOOKS PUBLISHING

FROG'S WINTER WALK

*In which Frog conducts an experiment,
wears a feather coat, and reveals the hidden mystery
of the coldest season of the year.*

Written by Jessica Schaub & Illustrated by Sarah Aman

Someone asked me once, "What do frogs do in the winter?"

Normally, the answer is, "Hibernate."

Frogs burrow down under the wet earth, fall into a deep sleep, and wait for spring.

But I am a frog with a taste for science and an inquisitive nature.

My good friend, Bird told me that many birds fly south in the winter and that Rabbit and Weasel turn white. Bird also said the earth turns white.

Flowers on my pond are white. The clouds are white. But I have never seen the whole earth white.

I had to see for myself if these things were true. I decided that this year I would not hibernate. I gathered leaves to make a field journal. Every great mind has a notebook in which to write down thoughts and ideas.

My Questions:

1. Do birds really go south for the winter?
2. Why would Rabbit and Weasel turn white during the winter?
3. What would cause the earth to turn white?
4. Bird tells me winter is cold. What is cold?
5. What will I need to do to prepare for winter?

July 23

I am a frog and frogs are not winter animals. Bird told me I would have to find a way to stay warm. Bird has feathers. Rabbit has thick fur. Frogs have mucus on our skin to protect us from the water, but mucus will not keep me warm.

To-do List for Winter:

1. Find a way to keep warm.

2. Find a place to sleep at night.

August 11

I gathered Bird's fallen feathers for a coat. If feathers keep Bird warm, they should work for me too.

Spider wove the feathers together into a coat.
I wore my coat for Bird and Spider.

August 20

Snake said I would need coverings for my feet. Using Snake's molted skin, Spider stitched a beautiful pair of boots. After I lined the boots with moss, Bird said my feet would be plenty warm.

October 5

This is going to be harder than I thought. I'm so tired and the air is getting colder. My head is also cold. Bird wove a tiny nest for my head. Spider made it waterproof with her webbing. With some of Bird's feathers tucked inside, I'm perfectly warm.

October 24

I was grateful to discover that winter days are shorter than summer days. With nights so long, I have more time to sleep each night to make up for missing hibernation. Each morning feels a little colder, but the world still is not white.

November 1

I woke to a gaggle of gathering geese. Our pond transformed from a placid pool to a rowdy ruckus of feathered friends.

Those geese sure can talk! All day long they discussed this pond, that lake, and which grass was the sweetest.

At noon, a stillness settled on the pond as they all looked skyward. Near the clouds, I saw giant arrows sailing through the air.

Like thunder, the geese beat their wings and launched upward. Within minutes the geese formed more arrows and followed the others.

I looked at Bird and smiled. The geese were going south.
I wished that my feathered coat would allow me to join them.

Novemburrrrr 21

Thought I saw a ghost today. Bird was right. Rabbits do turn white in the winter!

If I looked afraid of a white rabbit, then Rabbit's face was the same. He asked me what kind of fat bird I was. I told him I was a frog. I don't think Rabbit believed me.

December 21

Bird told the truth about everything. This morning, the ground was covered with white snow. At first, I thought the cottonwood trees had dropped their fluffy seeds again, but the snow is cold and wet.

Ode to the White Earth
by F. Pondswallow

To think that I should come to know
the wonders of fresh fallen snow.
Drifting softly, not a sound,
Crystal stars conceal the ground.
Along the pond white statues stand,
Oh, beauty of winter land!

January 3

Today I went sledding with otter...

...and I made snow frogs.

January 4

Now that I have seen winter, the migration of geese, Rabbit's white fur, and snow, I am tired. Deep at the base of bird's tree, I will burrow down under a thick blanket of fallen leaves.

Winter is beautiful, but I'm a frog. Summer is my season.

Free teacher resources for using *Frog's Winter Walk* in a classroom or homeschool are available at:

www.BooksByJessica.com

Want to see more of Frog and his friends? Visit the author's website above to see exclusive illustrations!

Made in the USA
Charleston, SC
09 September 2014